MW01153889

WITHDRAWN

THE DARK SIDE

Demons
and Ghouls

illustrated by David West
and
written by Anita Ganeri

PowerKiDS
press.
New York

Published in 2011 by The Rosen Publishing Group, Inc.
29 East 21st Street, New York, NY 10010

Copyright © 2011 David West Books

All rights reserved. No part of this book may be reproduced in any form without permission in writing from the publisher, except by a reviewer.

Designed and produced by
David West Books

Designer: Gary Jeffrey
Editor: Ronne Randall
U.S. Editor: Kara Murray
Illustrator: David West

Photographic credits: 18b, antwerpenR; 20t, Truthven; 21b, notacrime

Library of Congress Cataloging-in-Publication Data

Ganeri, Anita, 1961–
Demons and ghouls / by Antia Ganeri ; illustrated by David West. — 1st ed.
p. cm. — (The dark side)
Includes index.
ISBN 978-1-61531-896-4 (library binding) — ISBN 978-1-4488-1564-7 (pbk.) —
ISBN 978-1-4488-1565-4 (6-pack)
1. Demonology—Juvenile literature. I. West, David, 1956– II. Title.
BF1531.G36 2011
133.4'2—dc22

2010009111

Manufactured in China

CPSIA Compliance Information: Batch #DS0102PK: For Further Information contact Rosen Publishing, New York, New York at 1-800-237-9932

Contents

Introduction

Many bizarre and gruesome creatures roam the world of mythology. Their origins may be lost in the mists of history, but they have preyed on people's superstitions since ancient times. Among the most terrifying are demons, evil spirits that work for the powers of darkness against the powers of good. For centuries, people have believed in these hideous creatures that terrified and tormented their victims. Demons and devils also appear in many religions, using their powers to tempt people into wickedness. But demons are not the only evil spirits. There are also ghouls, imps, elves, and goblins. Are you ready to go over to the dark side? It will send shivers down your spine . . .

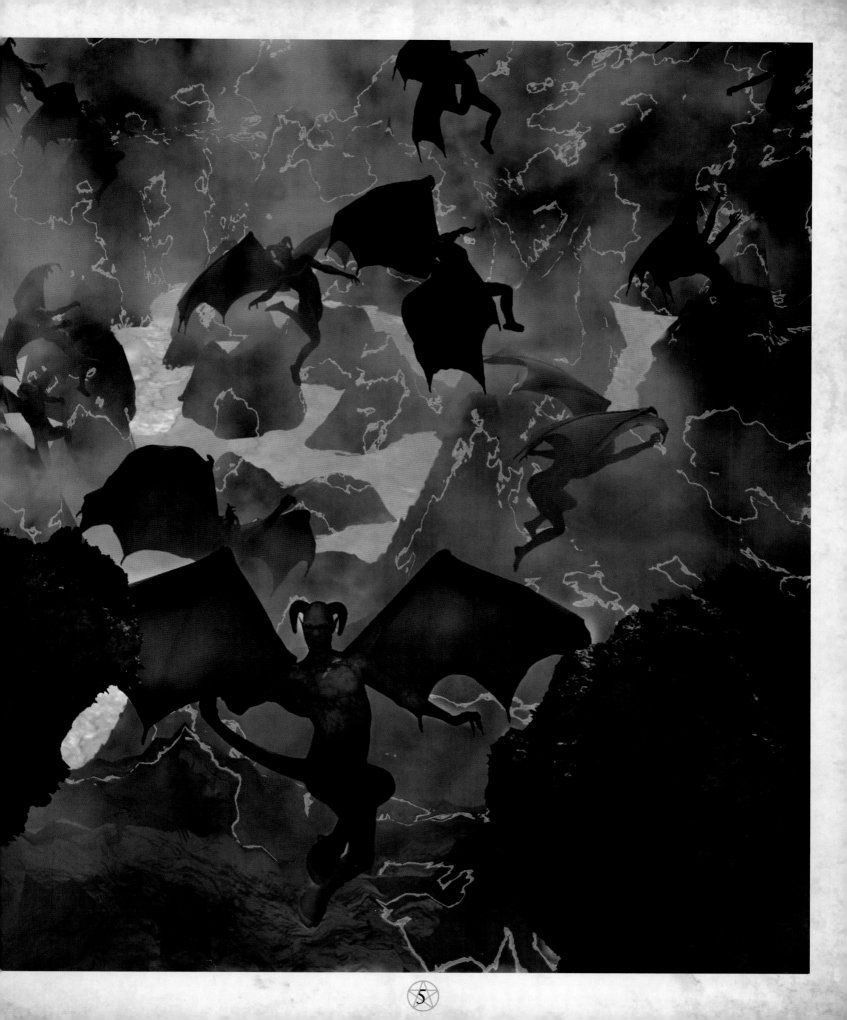

Demons

Rising from its underground realm of fire, a terrible winged and horned figure heads for the world of the living. It is a demon, on its way to wreak havoc in the lives of mortals.

Buer appears in Pseudomonarchia Daemonuma, *a sixteenth-century magician's handbook of demons. He is known as the Great President of Hell.*

A demon is a supernatural being from the dark side. Demons are found and feared in many religions and cultures around the world. Their evil work includes fighting the gods and tormenting people in hell but mostly they possess the living and make them act against their will. The word "demon" comes from the Greek *daimon*, meaning supernatural being or spirit.

In ancient Roman mythology, Charon carries the dead to the underworld, over the rivers Styx and Acheron. He is often shown as a demon.

The Devil—the worst demon.

Demonic Features

Demons come in all shapes and sizes, but they are almost always hideous and terrifying creatures. Batlike wings, horns, and razor-sharp claws are common demonic features.

Demons can appear in human form, as part human, or as part animal (bats, dogs, cats, and goats are popular animal forms for demons). Some can shape-shift between human and animal form, or between different animal forms.

Horns seem to be almost compulsory for demons! Here is a horned Japanese oni.

Demons can be tiny, or they can be gigantic. Besides horns and wings, their features often include oversized hands and feet, wide-open eyes, pointed ears, and red or blue skin. Multiple heads and limbs are also common.

The Grand Marquis of Hell, part wolf, part griffon, part serpent. It also spits fire.

Many demons are a bizarre mixture of different wild beasts, often with some human features mixed in. One example is the Christian demon known as the Grand Marquis of Hell. It has the body of a wolf, the wings of a griffon (a griffon is a mythical creature that is part eagle and part lion), and the tail of a serpent.

Two fierce demons torment a victim. One appears to be part human, part bat, the other has claws and a goat's head.

This frightening drawing shows Saint Anthony being
plagued by a host of hideous demons. The demons take the form
of fantastic wild creatures with human and animal features.

Possessed by Demons

Since ancient times, people from many cultures and followers of many religions have believed that they can be possessed by demons. The only way to cast out the demon is exorcism.

Strange behavior, loss of memory, shrieking, groaning, garbled speech, superhuman strength, fainting, and seizures are all characteristics of a person taken over by a demon. The ancient Sumerians were one of many ancient peoples who believed in sickness demons. They prayed for protection from them.

Saint Benedict, who was born in Italy in AD 480, exorcising a demon. Today, a Saint Benedict Medal (or Saint Benedict Cross) is used to ward off demons. It carries the words "Begone Satan."

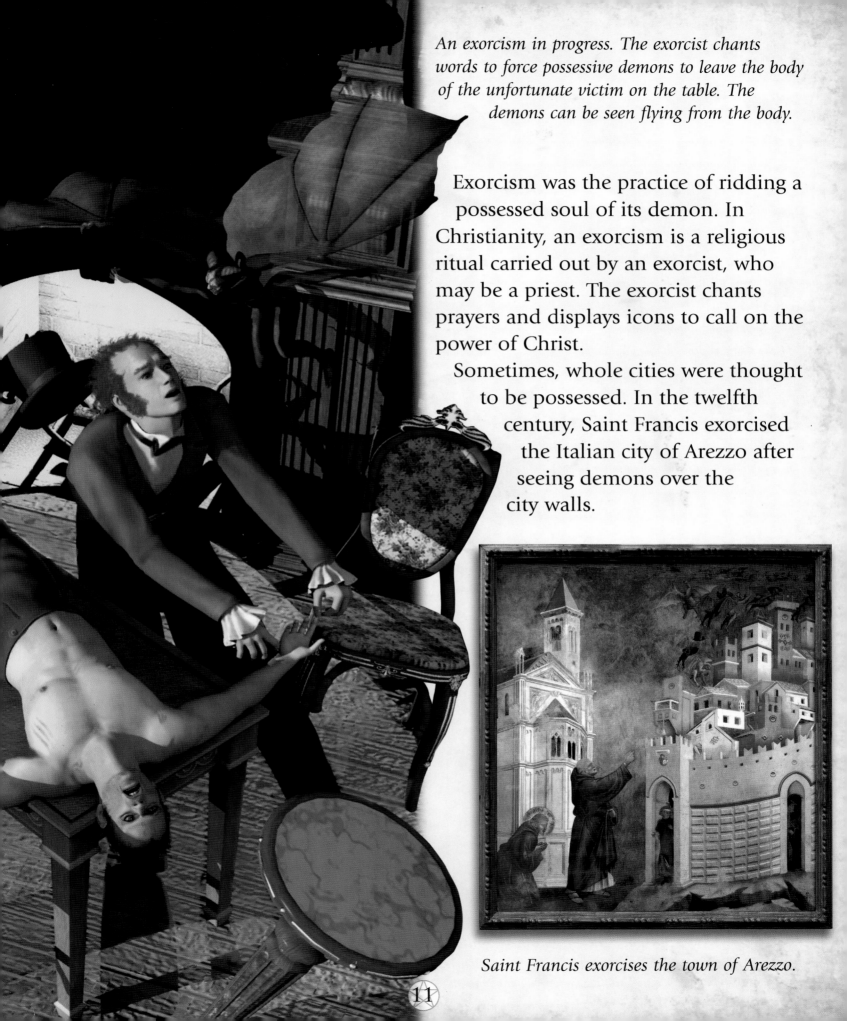

An exorcism in progress. The exorcist chants words to force possessive demons to leave the body of the unfortunate victim on the table. The demons can be seen flying from the body.

Exorcism was the practice of ridding a possessed soul of its demon. In Christianity, an exorcism is a religious ritual carried out by an exorcist, who may be a priest. The exorcist chants prayers and displays icons to call on the power of Christ.

Sometimes, whole cities were thought to be possessed. In the twelfth century, Saint Francis exorcised the Italian city of Arezzo after seeing demons over the city walls.

Saint Francis exorcises the town of Arezzo.

Demons in Judaism and Christianity

This is Belphegor—in Christianity, the chief demon of the deadly sin of sloth (laziness).

Many stories of demons are written down in the Jewish and Christian holy books, the Tanakh and the Bible. These demons are always evil, attempting to lead people into sinful ways against the teachings of their religion.

In both Judaism and Christianity, demons are fallen angels—spirits that were once angels but have moved to the dark side. The demons were close to God in heaven but tried to become too powerful and were punished by being thrown out. They try to retaliate by tempting people into doing evil, against God's wishes.

In the Bible, Jesus cures sick people by casting demons out of their bodies. And in the Middle Ages, members of the Christian Church believed that witchcraft was demon worship.

The demon Apollyon (also known as Abbadon) battles the hero Christian in John Bunyan's The Pilgrim's Progress.

Various Christian scholars have tried to classify demons. Some tried grouping them by their powers, and some by the sins they encourage. In 1589, Peter Binsfeld named the demons for each of the seven deadly sins (for example, Lucifer was the demon of pride, and Satan the demon of anger). Two of the major demons of Judaism are Azazel and Lilith. Azazel is the goatlike demon of the wilderness and uncleanliness. Lilith is the female demon of the night.

Azazel is a Hebrew devil who is a fallen angel. Here he takes the form of a demonic goat, led by a second demon.

In Judaism, the night demon Lilith is the bringer of storms, illness, and other terrible things. She is sometimes known as the queen of the demons. She always appears with wings and long, flowing hair.

Demons in Islam

In Islam, there are angels, humans, and jinni. The jinni, or genies, are demons. But unlike the demons of Christianity and Judaism, jinni are not always evil.

Jinni live on Earth, alongside humans. They make their homes in stones, trees, and other earthly objects, usually in remote places. They even have their own jinni communities. Jinni can be benevolent (good and helpful) or malevolent (bad and menacing). The malevolent ones harass and sometimes possess humans. Muslims believe that every person has an evil jinni that tries to lead him astray. The jinni are said to have been created from "smokeless fire" by Allah, 2,000 years before the creation of Adam. Iblis, the Devil figure of Islam, is a type of jinni.

A jinni materializes in front of Aladdin, the hero of a popular story from The Thousand and One Nights. *This jinni is a demon that must obey its master's wishes.*

A stone relief of a winged genie from the palace of King Sargon of Assyria. It was carved about 715 BC, 1,500 years before Islam was founded. In Assyria, genies were thought of as protectors of the king.

Jinni appear in many forms—as animals such as snakes and dragons and also as humans when they need to trick people. They can be visible or invisible. These powers make jinni popular figures in folktales, such as the stories from *The Thousand and One Nights*.

An afrit (or efreeti) *is an unpleasant type of jinni that takes the form of a giant human. Here, an afrit overpowers a nobleman.*

The Devil

In many religions and cultures, the Devil is the most powerful of all the demons. The Devil is evil brought to life, the enemy of both God and good.

The red-bodied demon Ukobach is one of Beelzebub's helpers. His job is to feed fuel into the infernal boilers of hell.

In Christianity and Judaism, the Devil is a fallen angel, cast out of heaven for challenging the power of God. He is also known as Satan (the Prince of Devils), Lucifer (the Fallen Angel of Light), and Beelzebub (the Lord of the Flies). He is the leader of the other fallen angels. The Devil's job is to tempt humans into evil ways—to lead them away from God.

A medieval stained-glass panel shows the Devil on horseback leading people into evil ways.

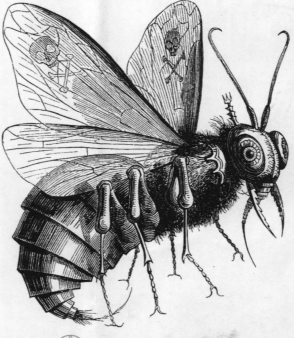

In Islam, the Devil is known as Iblis, the Demon, and the Enemy of God. Iblis was punished by Allah for not bowing in front of Adam, the first human, whom Allah had just created.

This is the demon Beelzebub, Lord of the Flies, as shown in a nineteenth-century book. The name has become an alternative name for the Devil.

Lucifer falls from heaven to hell. Sometimes Lucifer
is the name of the angel who was thrown down from heaven to become the
Devil. In Latin, Lucifer is another name for the planet Venus, the morning star.

Demons in Hinduism

In Hindu mythology, demonlike creatures appear in the guise of all manner of beasts. They include types of demon called *rakshasas*, *asuras*, and *vetalas*.

The rakshasas are shape-shifting demons that live on Earth. They possess people, terrify people, feed on human flesh, and spoil graves. They are capable of doing magic tricks and are great warriors. Their bodily features include poisonous fingernails. Among the rakshasas is the ten-headed demon Ravana, who appears in the *Ramayana*, an epic poem.

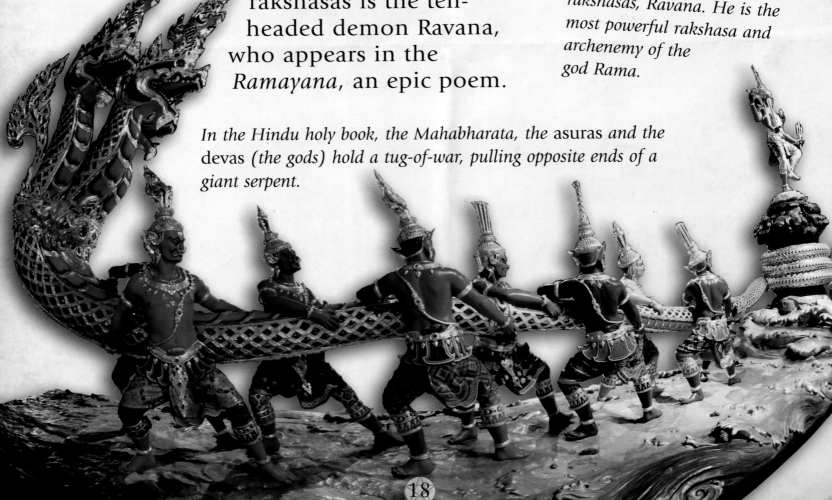

The ten-headed king of the rakshasas, Ravana. He is the most powerful rakshasa and archenemy of the god Rama.

In the Hindu holy book, the Mahabharata, the asuras and the devas (the gods) hold a tug-of-war, pulling opposite ends of a giant serpent.

Vetalas are hostile spirits of the dead, trapped between this life and the afterlife. They are batlike creatures that haunt cremation sites and possess corpses to walk from place to place.

A statue of the asura Mahishasura

The asuras are hideous demons who are in constant conflict with the gods, from whom they want to take power. They appear in human form and are mortal. Asuras have all the negative qualities that humans can have—pride, arrogance, anger, and ignorance.

The demon Mahishasura is the son of the king of asuras. He can shape-shift from human form into a water buffalo. He cannot be defeated in battle, either by man or by god. In myth, Mahishasura invaded heaven and kicked out all the gods, who then created a female goddess to kill him.

Demons Around the World

Demons appear not only in the religious stories of Christianity, Islam, Judaism, and Hinduism, but also in ancient cultures from China, Japan, and the Americas.

Extraordinary rock carvings depicting demons incurring the wrath of the Devil. The carvings, at Dazu in China, were made around 1,000 years ago.

The terrifying Japanese demon called an oni is a giant, unpleasant creature shown here with several eyes.

Japanese folklore features demons called *oni*. They can be benevolent but are generally cruel and nasty. Oni are normally ogres (giant creatures with great strength). Their features include three toes on their feet and three fingers on their hands. On their hairy heads are horns and many eyes. Their skin is reddish or bluish in color. Oni are very popular subjects in Japanese art.

More evidence of demons in Asia comes from Buddhist art. The demons are spirits that try to prevent people from achieving enlightenment. Among them is Mara, the Lord of Death. Mara sent armies of demonic monsters to attack the Buddha.

The *wendigo* is a demonic creature in the traditional beliefs of the Algonquian peoples of North America. It was also a cannibal, greedy for human flesh. It could possess people and was associated with hunger and starvation. It was said that a person could turn into a wendigo if she engaged in cannibalism.

A five-headed Buddhist demon carving in Thailand

The Native American demon the wendigo is a hideous sight. It is skeletal, with taut, gray skin over its bones. It carries the smell of death and decay, like a dead body that has been dug up!

21

Gods & Demons

Demons often represent evil in the struggle against good, which is represented by the gods. The conflict leads to terrible fights in which demons and gods pit their supernatural powers against each other.

In Christianity and Islam, the archangel Michael is leader of the angels and chief of the Army of God. It was Michael who cast Satan and the other fallen angels out of heaven.

The Hindu demon Ravana battles Rama after kidnapping Rama's wife, Sita.

The asuras (one of the types of demons) and devas (the gods) come to blows in many stories from Hindu mythology. In the epic poem the *Ramayana*, Ravana, a ten-headed demon, fights the god Rama.

22

Angra Mainyu, the Persian demon of darkness, plunging to his death. Flying above is the god Ahura Mazda, who has beaten Angra Mainyu in battle. The fight takes place at the end of time.

Persian mythology features an epic battle between good and evil. On one side was Ahura Mazda, the supreme god, creator of the heavens and Earth, the power of goodness and light. On the other was Angra Mainyu (or Ahriman), the god of darkness, the destroyer of good and the creator of evil.

The Martyr Nikita was a fourth-century Goth (the Goths were a Germanic tribe). He helped spread Christianity through Europe and killed a few demons along the way.

The Martyr Nikita about to kill a demon in his quest to spread Christianity

Other Evil Spirits

Stomping through the woods comes a hairy creature with the head of a black goat. This is just one of the many terrifying forms taken up by the *pooka*—the most feared of the Irish fairy folk.

In German folklore, the mare is the spirit that brings nightmares.

The pooka, who scoops up travelers and throws them in bogs, is one of numerous types of evil spirits. Most are not as harmful as the demons but nonetheless create trouble and chaos in their own ways. They include the ghouls, the imps, the elves and goblins, the mares of German folklore, and the Japanese *tengu*.

From Japanese folklore comes the tengu, a dangerous spirit of the countryside. Here is one caught by an elephant.

Ghouls

The ghoul is one of the nastiest supernatural beings. Ghouls originate in Arabian folklore. They are said to live in cemeteries and other uninhabited places, where they live on the flesh of the dead.

A ghoul is a devilish sort of demon or jinni from Arabian folklore. It is the offspring of Iblis, Islam's Devil figure. Ghouls were said to live in the desert, tricking unfortunate travelers by shape-shifting, then killing and eating them.

A hungry ghoulish grave robber takes a dead body from its resting place.

The ghouls of Arabian folklore were said to possess bodies of hyenas, perhaps because these animals also feed on dead animals.

The graveyard is a favorite place for ghouls. There is a regular supply of dead human flesh there.

The earliest stories in history that feature ghouls are in the famous collection of Arabian stories *The Thousand and One Nights*. For example, in the "The History of Gherib and His Brother Agib," Gherib, a prince, fights hungry ghouls who want to eat him, captures them, and converts them to Islam.

Because of their taste for human flesh, ghouls and similar evil spirits are popular creatures in modern horror fiction, movies, and video games. In some stories, they are humanlike figures. In others, they are terrible beasts. Ghouls are sometimes confused with zombies, which are mindless corpses.

Imps, Elves, and Goblins

A gargoyle in the shape of an imp

There is an assortment of peculiar tiny spirits that spread chaos and mischief throughout mythology.

The lively imp enjoys playing practical jokes. Imps are often seen as the familiars (helpers) of witches. Elves are originally from Germanic folklore and appear in the form of miniature humans. Elves make trouble by stealing human children and by causing nightmares and disease. Dwarfs come from Scandinavian mythology. They are industrious creatures that live inside mountains and mines. Normally harmless, they become nasty if crossed.

A cobbler dwarf

Throughout Europe, fairy rings were supposed to be places where elves gathered, or a doorway to the kingdom of the elves. In reality, they are naturally occurring rings of fungi.

28

Goblins feature in western European folklore. One version of their story says they spread from Britain to live all over Europe. They are small, with wrinkled skin and pointy ears. They cause trouble in homes at night, making noise, moving furniture around, and taking pajamas off sleeping people. It is said that they also help punish naughty children in some homes!

Goblins are often troublemakers in children's fairy tales.

The brownie of Scottish folklore was a small fairy that helped with housework but sometimes made a mess. Hobgoblins were similar to brownies. They were small, hairy men who were annoying but friendly and who would do jobs in return for food.

A boggart at his mischievous work, creating chaos by stealing and moving things. Boggarts are found in northern England.

Glossary

archangel (AHRK-ayn-jel) One of the main, or chief, angels.

benevolent (beh-NEV-lent) Good and helpful.

Buddhist (BOO-dist) Linked to the religious beliefs of Buddhism, a faith that began in India in the sixth century BC.

cannibal (KA-nih-bul) A human who eats the flesh of other human beings.

Christianity (kris-chee-A-nih-tee) A religion based on the teachings of Jesus Christ, who lived in the Middle East around 2,000 years ago.

classify (KLA-seh-fy) To arrange or put into order.

cremation (krih-MAY-shun) Burning a dead body to ashes.

enlightenment (en-LY-ten-ment) In Buddhist beliefs, when a person suddenly realizes the truth.

exorcism (EK-sawr-sih-zum) A ritual held to get rid of an evil spirit or demon from a person or place.

folklore (FOHK-lawr) Traditional stories and tales from a place or culture.

Hinduism (HIN-doo-ih-zum) An ancient religion practiced by millions of people who live in or originate from India.

icons (EYE-konz) Images or pictures of Jesus Christ or of a saint.

Islam (IS-lom) A religion taught by Muhammad in Arabia in the seventh century AD. Its followers are called Muslims.

Judaism (JOO-dee-ih-zum) A religion that began thousands of years ago in the Middle East. Its followers are called Jews.

malevolent (muh-LEH-vuh-lent) Bad and menacing.

mythology (mih-THAH-luh-jee) Traditional stories, not based in historical fact, and using supernatural characters to explain human behavior and events.

shape-shift (SHAYP-shift) To change form from human to animal, animal to human, or animal to animal.

supernatural (soo-per-NA-chuh-rul) Magical beings, like fairies, ghosts, and elves, and unexplained events.

Further Reading

Allen, Judy, et al. *Fantasy Encyclopedia.* Boston: Kingfisher, 2005.

Ganeri, Anita. *An Illustrated Guide to Mythical Creatures.* New York: Hammond, 2009.

Matthew, Caitlin and John. *The Element Encyclopedia of Magical Creatures.* New York: Sterling, 2005.

McNab, Chris. *Mythical Monsters: The Scariest Creatures from Legends, Books, and Movies.* New York: Tangerine Press, 2006.

Thirteenth-century Italian mosaic of hell

Index

Web Sites

Due to the changing nature of Internet links, PowerKids Press has developed an online list of Web sites related to the subject of this book. This site is updated regularly. Please use this link to access the list:
www.powerkidslinks.com/darkside/demons/